Sophia Learns to Pray

Shelby Turner

www.thedailygraceco.com

Unless otherwise noted, Scripture quotations have been taken from the Christian Standard Bible®, Copyright © 2020 by Holman Bible Publishers. Used by permission. Christian Standard Bible® and CSB® are federally registered trademarks of Holman Bible Publishers.

Designed in the United States of America and printed in China.

STUDY CONTRIBUTORS

Illustrator:
KATIE GRACE WILL

Editors:
HELEN HUMMEL
ALLI TURNER
JENNIE HEIDEMAN

When the sun floods her room,
and she first starts to wake,
Sophia springs up in bed!
What adventures await!

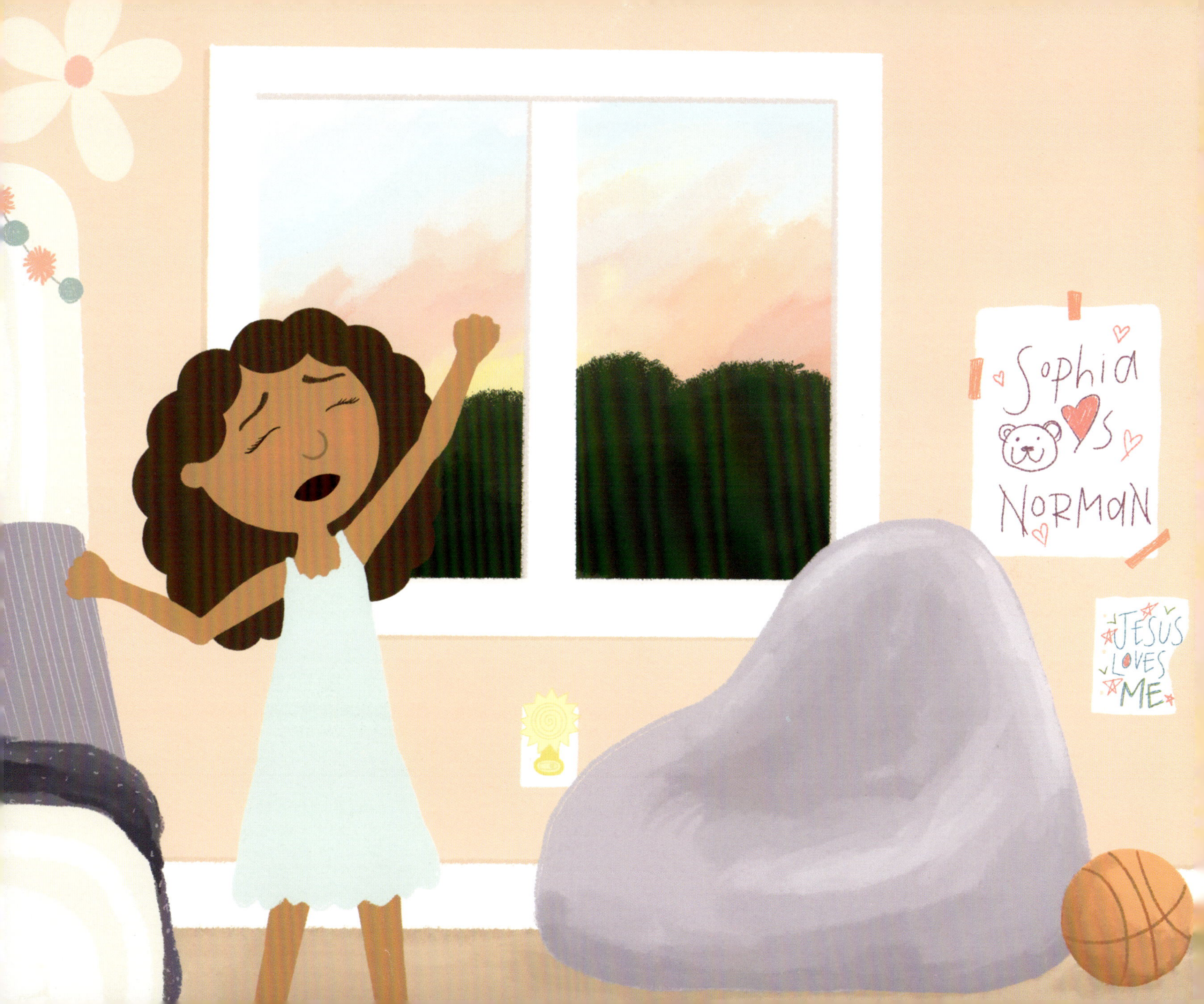
Sophia ♥s
NORMAN
JESUS
LOVES
ME

Some days she blasts into space.
Others she stays on the ground.
No matter where she ventures,
Norman is always around.

He is fluffy and squishy
and has the cutest pink nose.
He gives big, cozy bear hugs
and goes wherever she goes.

But then, just right before bed,
Norman is missing, lost, gone.

Oh me. Oh my. No, no, NO! "It can't be," Sophia yawned.

Dad searched outside and in.
He had looked everywhere.
With hands empty, he said,
"This is a time for prayer."

Sobs. Sniffles. Sad, sad tears.
"Prayer?" Sophia whimpered.
"Yes," Dad leaned in closer.
He hugged her and whispered.

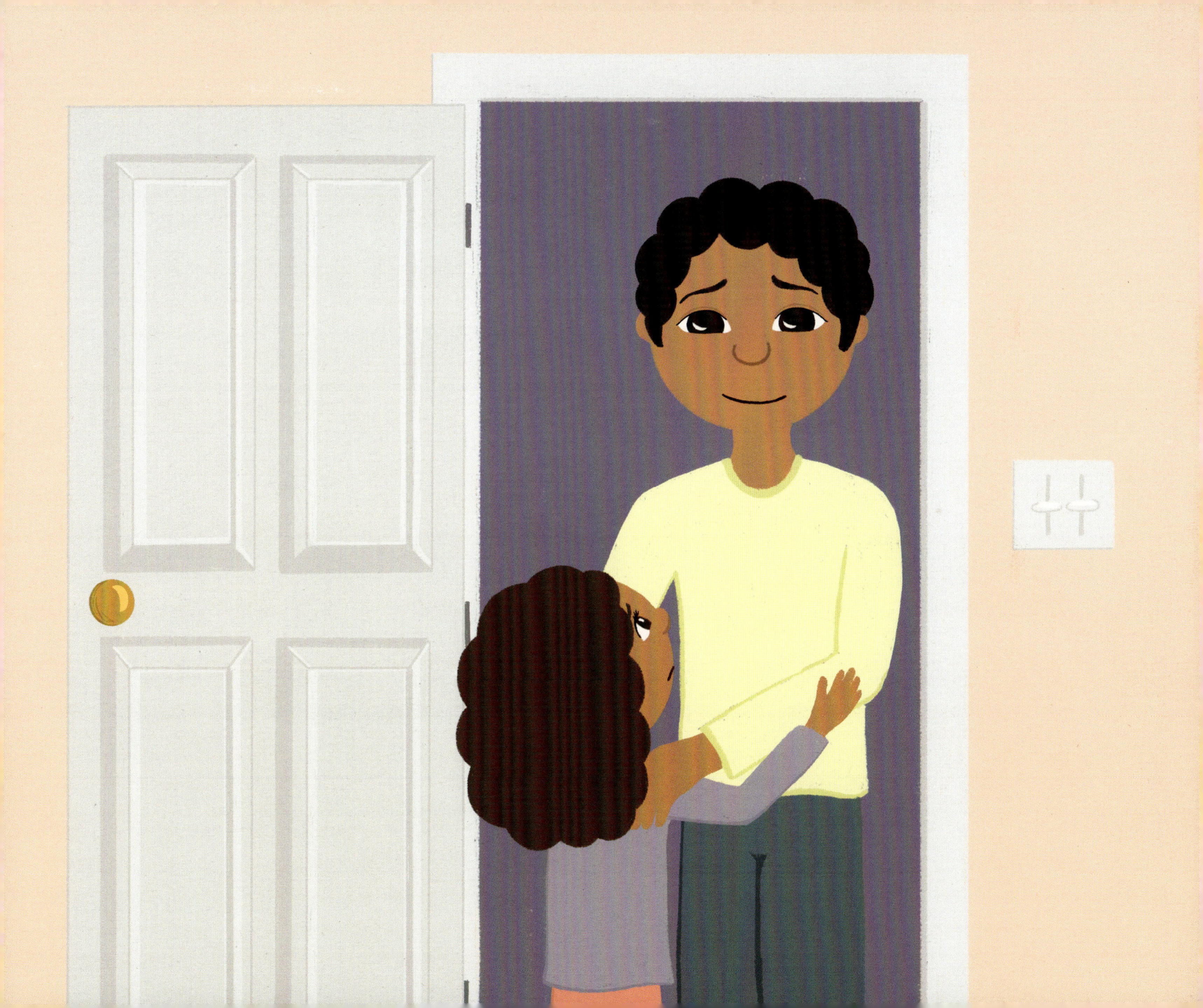

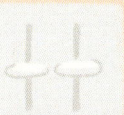

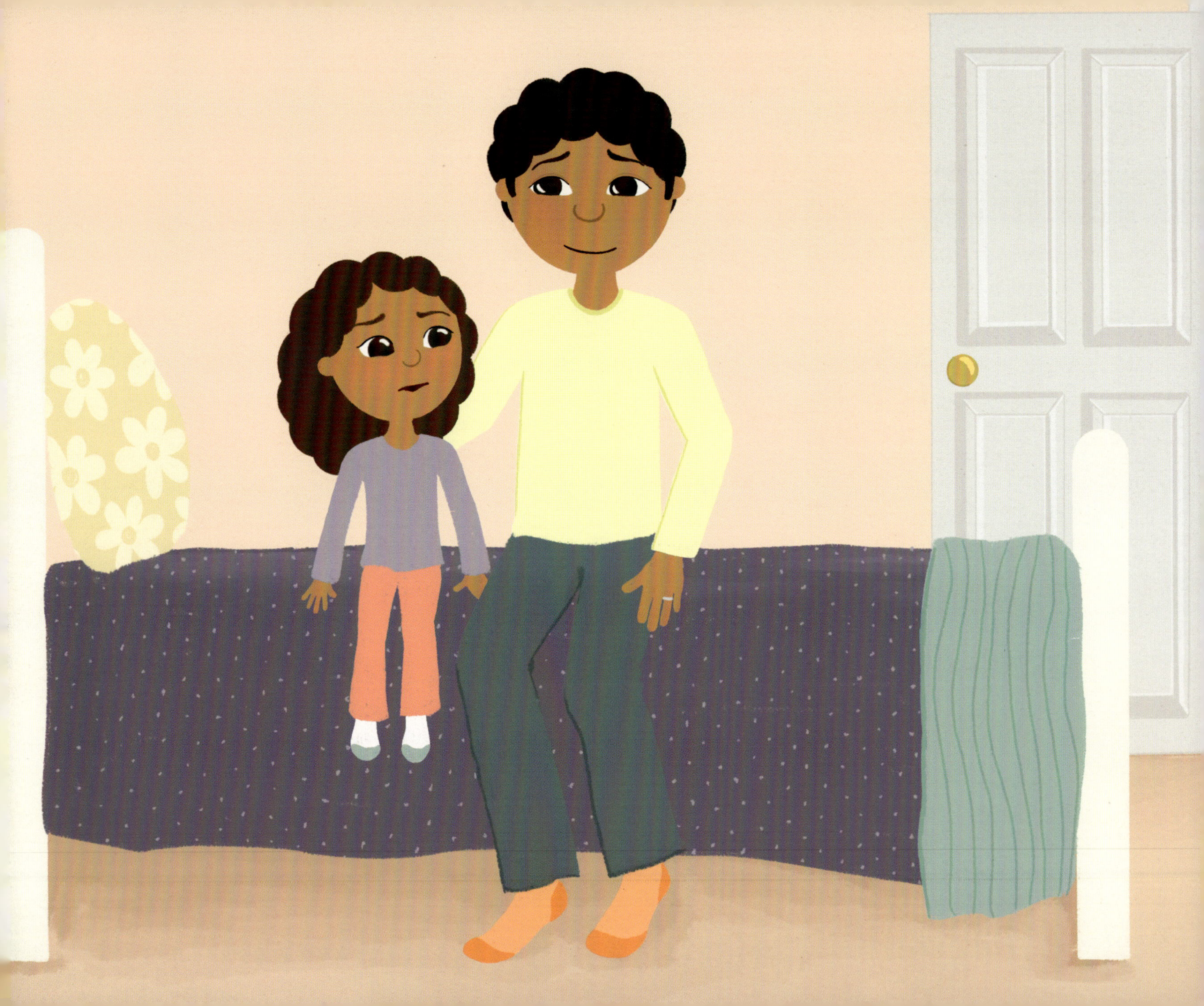

"When we have a need,
a thought, or a wish,
God wants us to share
from our heart to His."

"Prayer is a gift God
gives us to stay near.
Though we can't see Him,
we know that He hears."

"We can talk to God
when we're sick or sad,
hopeful or excited,
or sorry or glad."

"God knows all things about you
yet still carefully listens.
When you pray, He will answer
each and every petition."

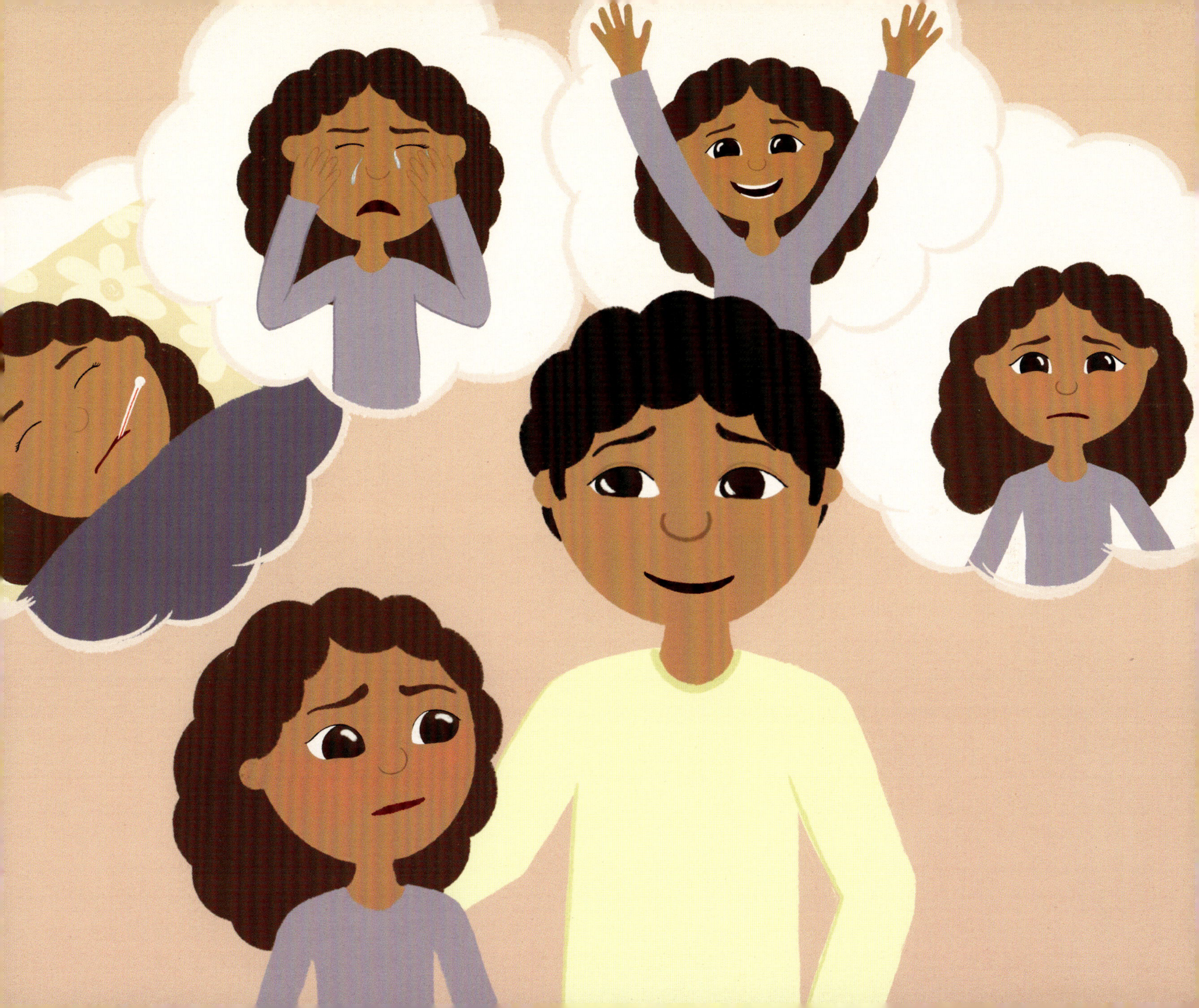

"He knows where Norman is
and how to find him, too.
Let's stop and pray right now
that God will help you through."

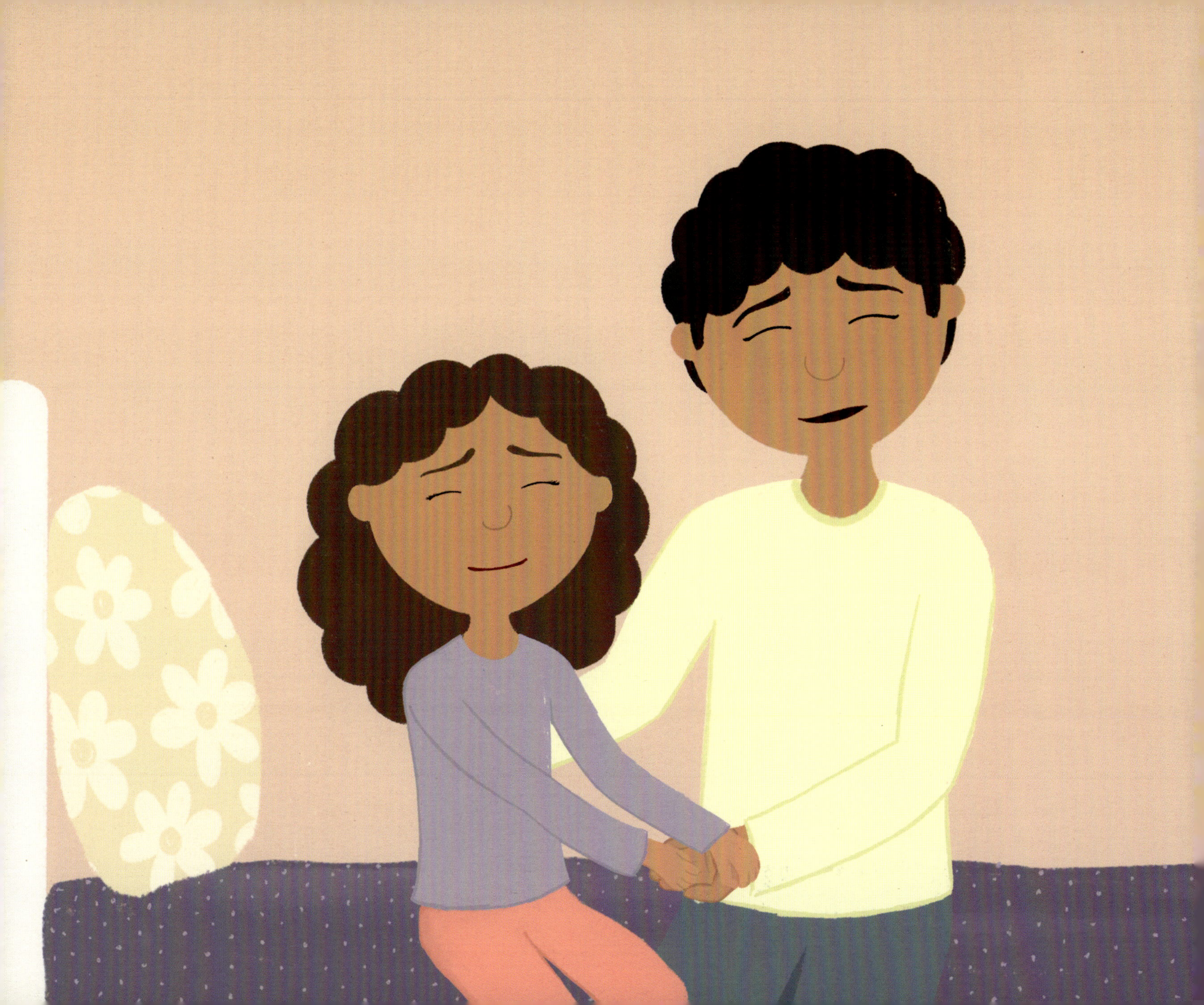

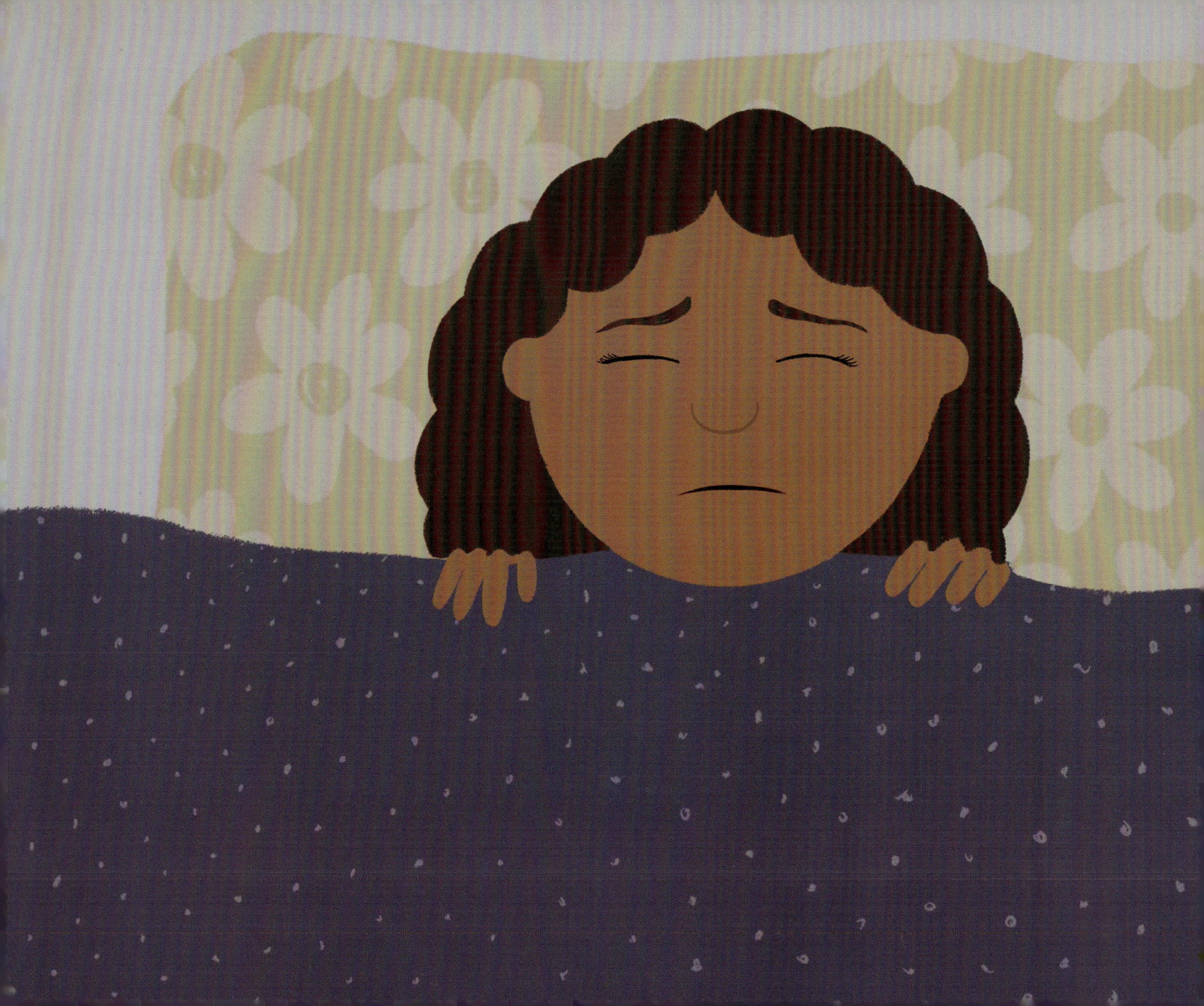

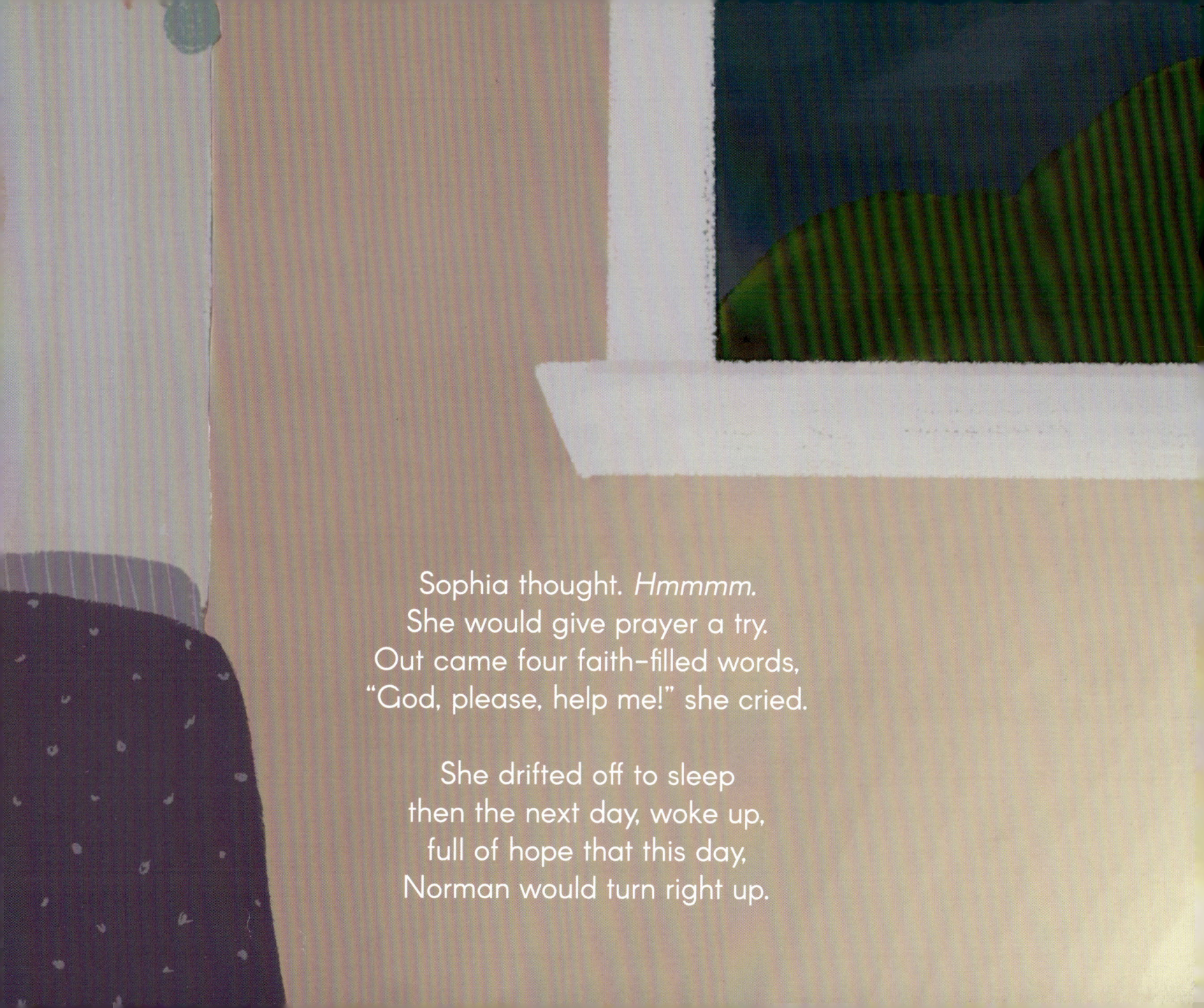

Sophia thought. *Hmmmm.*
She would give prayer a try.
Out came four faith-filled words,
"God, please, help me!" she cried.

She drifted off to sleep
then the next day, woke up,
full of hope that this day,
Norman would turn right up.

She looked for dear Norman
around school and at home,
during dinner and bath,
and while her hair was combed.

But there was no Norman.

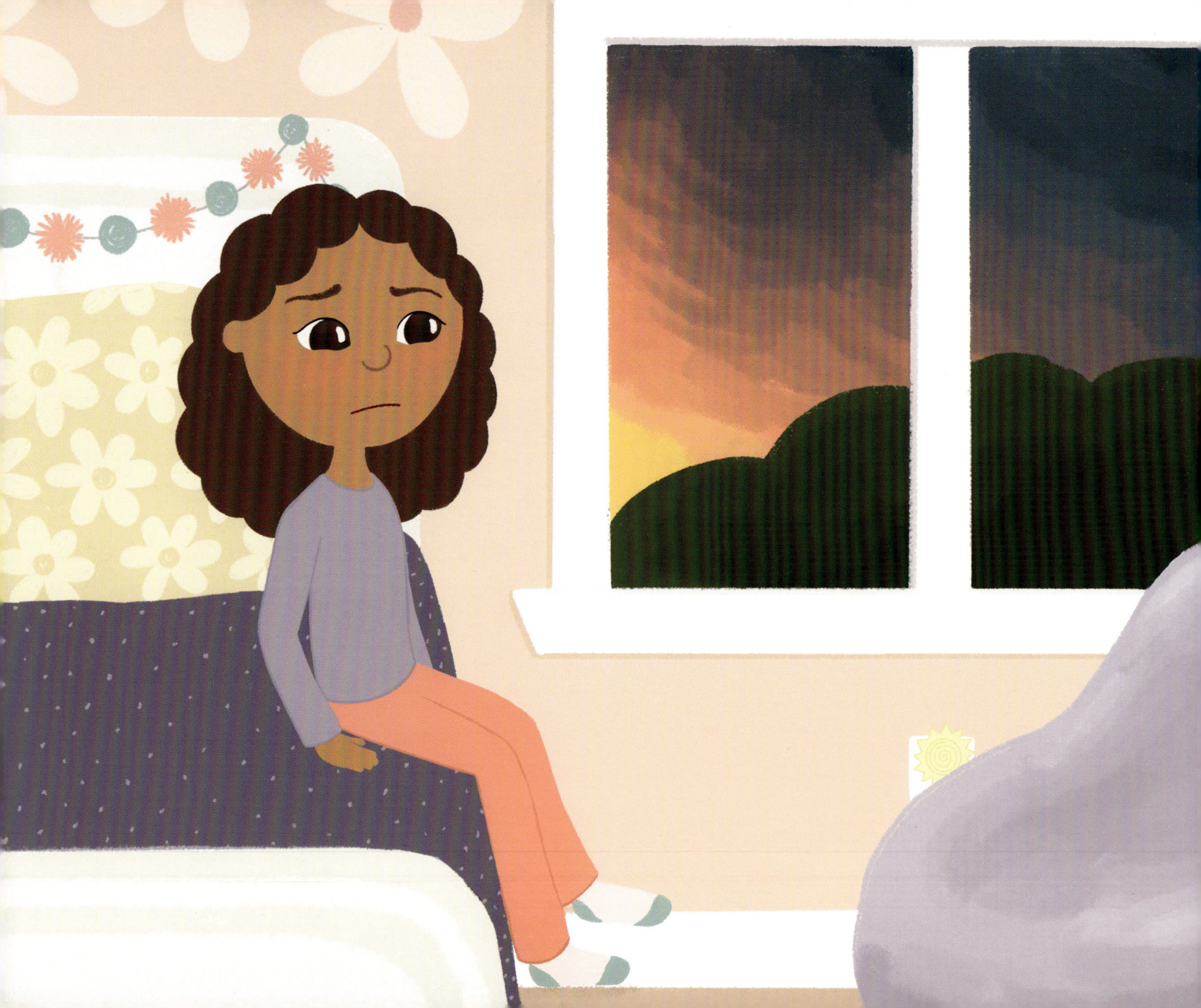

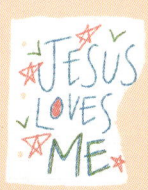

And even worse, much worse,
as bedtime neared,
a loud, rumbling rainstorm
suddenly appeared.

What would Sophia do now?
Norman always helped her sleep
when the wind blew and whistled
and when the thunder boomed deep.

Dad gave Sophia a hug.
Softly, he started to pray,
"God, please bring Norman home.
And help Sophia sleep today."

Sophia wasn't sure these prayers were working.

Did He hear?

Did God care?

Was God there?

Was He near?

As Sophia snuggled in bed thinking these rather big thoughts,
she noticed the loud, rumbly storm didn't have her tummy in knots.

"Goodness gracious," she thought. What unusual peace!
From where was this calm? Did God help her fear cease?

Embraced by God's comfort, she drifted off to sleep
with no worry or care and a newfound belief.

Perhaps God did hear her prayers. Maybe what Dad said was true.
God had not brought Norman back, but could He have a plan there, too?

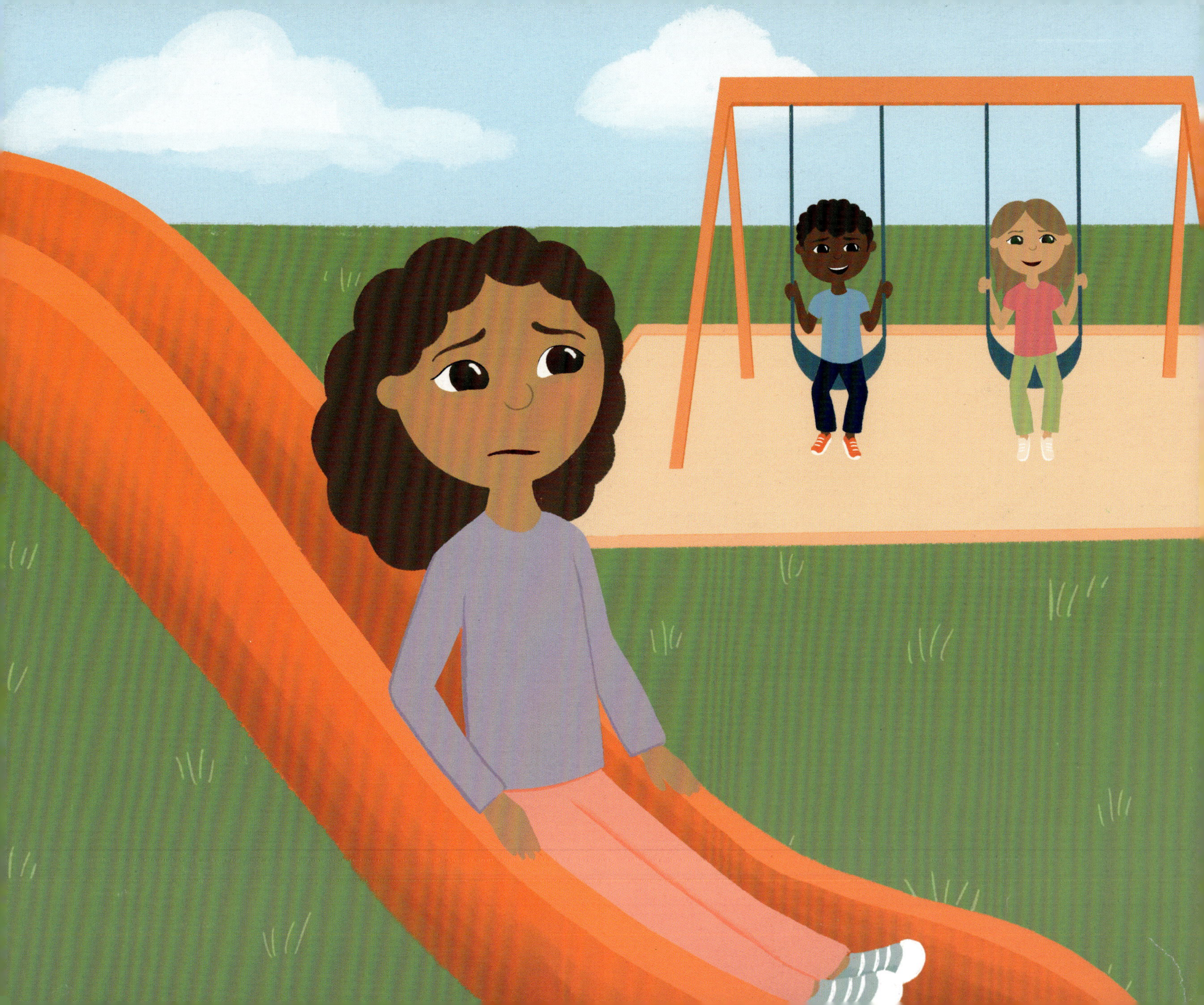

The next morning at school,
she decided to pray
for her bear to come home,
to be found, to find a way.

She prayed...

sitting at her desk,
walking down the hall,
on the slide at recess,
and in the bathroom stall.

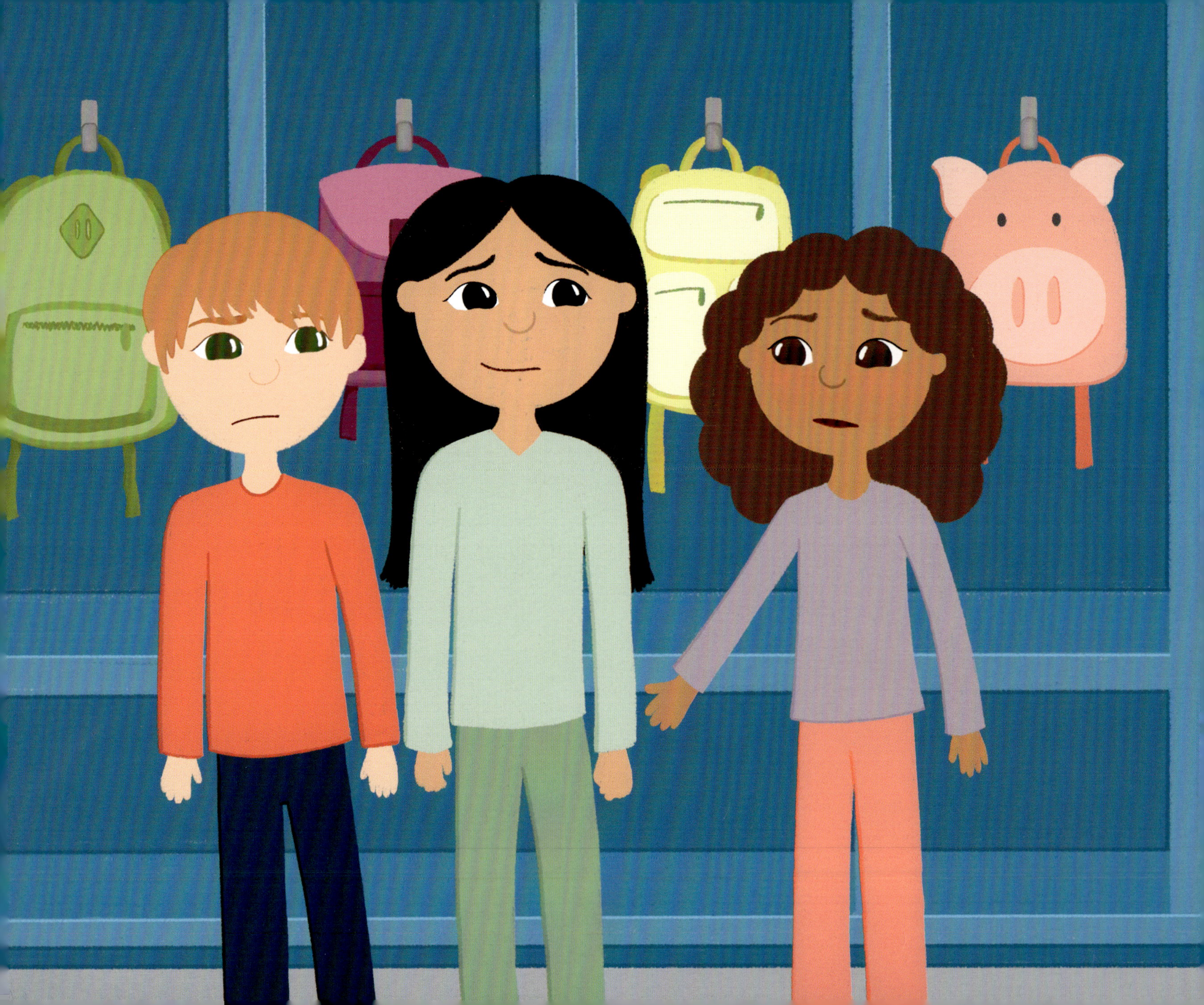

She prayed while she read
and while she ate lunch.
She asked friends to pray, too.
Sophia prayed SO MUCH.

At the end of the day,
she was saddened to see
her prayers went unanswered
Until so suddenly...

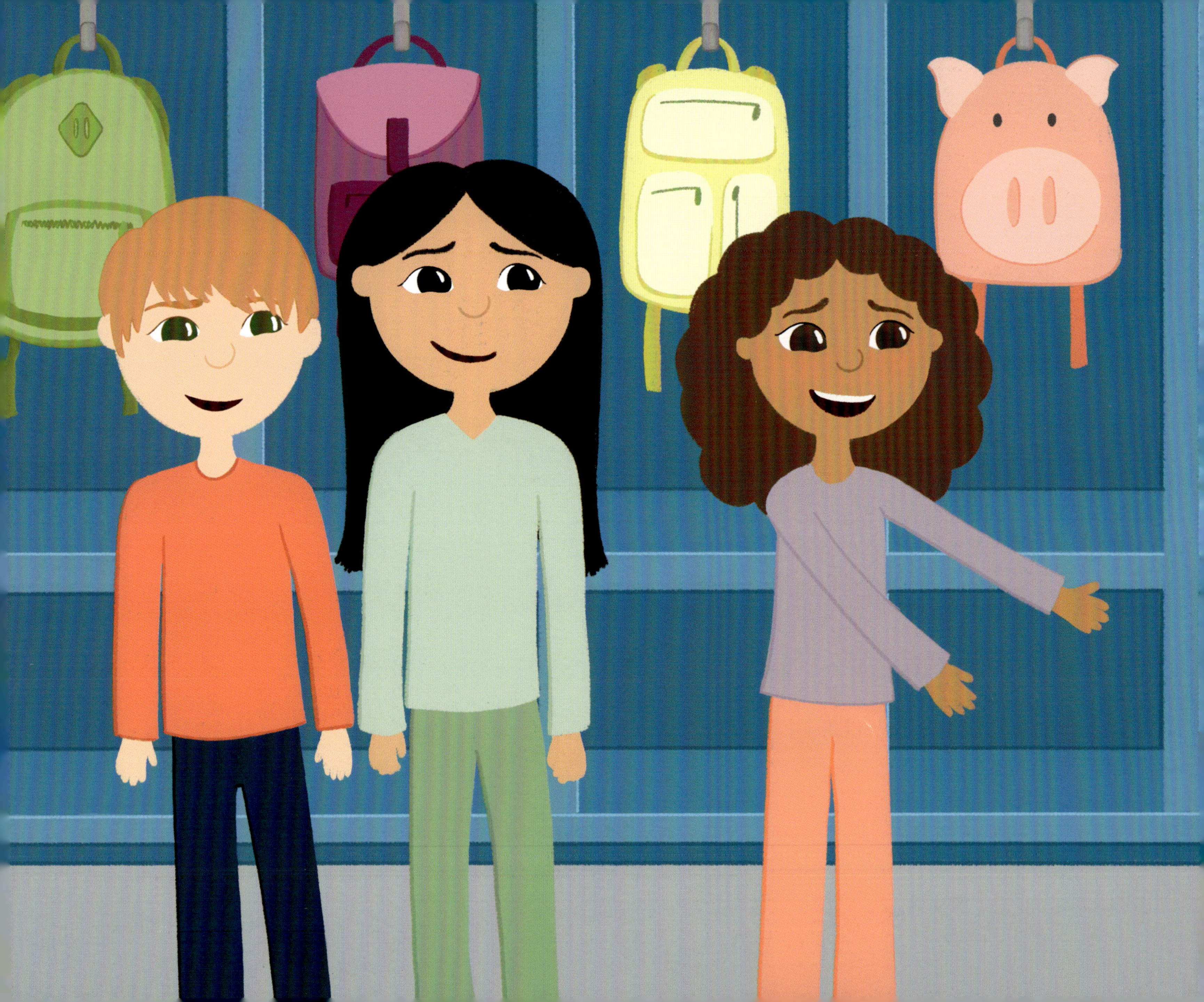

Up walked soccer coach James.
And what was he holding?
Sophia couldn't believe
how this all was unfolding!

Norman!!

She squeezed Norman so tight
and gave him a big kiss.
By mistake she'd left him
at her soccer practice.

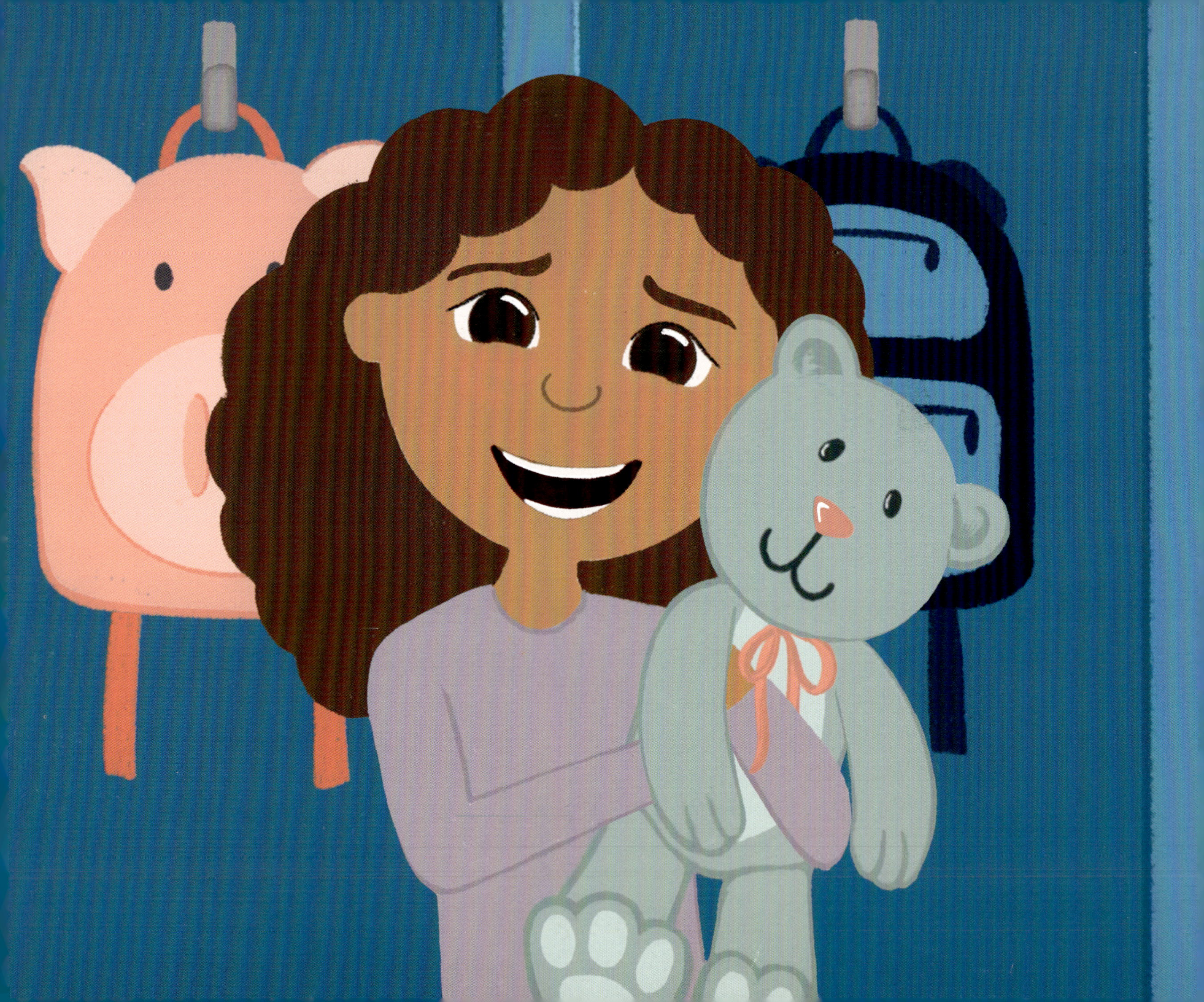

Sophia was relieved.
Her best buddy was back!
But she was also surprised
how God worked while she lacked.

While Norman was gone,
she learned how to pray.
She had felt God's peace,
learned to trust His way.

God had graciously answered
her prayers with a "yes."
But she could still trust Him
if He said "no" or "not yet."

God answers all our prayers
in the right time and way.
Even when we must wait
to hear what He will say.

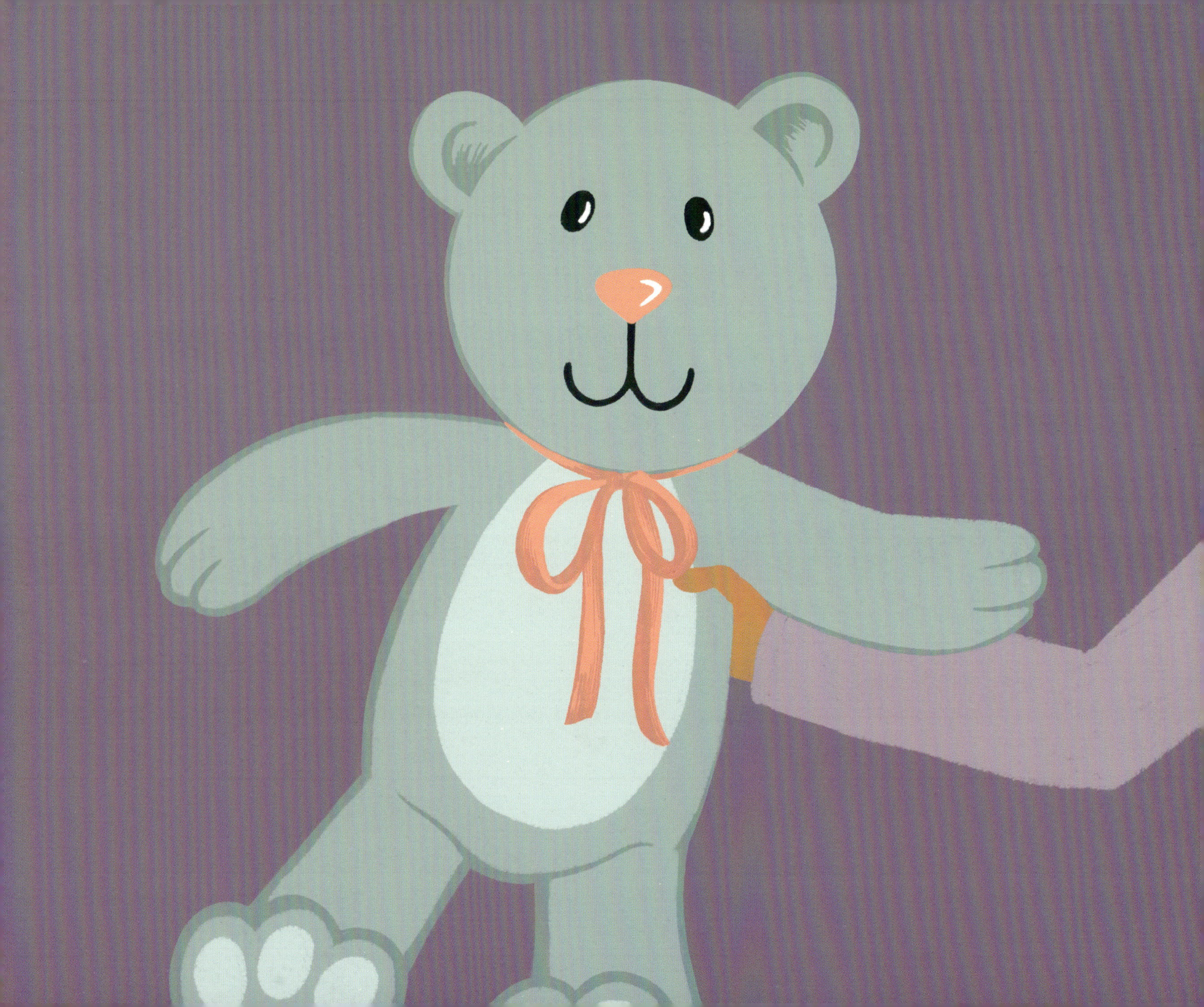

Sophia knew better now what prayer was all about. It was about her and God connecting heart to heart.

In an odd sort of way,
she was glad for this strife.
For now, she understood
prayer was a gift in her life.

Prayer is a gift
God gives to you, too.
He loves you dearly.
God wants to hear you.

Before you close this book,
Take one minute to pray.
And know that you can trust
each and every day...

God is there.

He does hear.

God does care.

He is near.

What is the Gospel?

THE WORD "GOSPEL" MEANS "GOOD NEWS."

The gospel is the most beautiful story in the whole world! God created the world and everything in it and made it good. He also made people, and He loved them very much.

BUT THE PEOPLE DISOBEYED GOD. THIS IS CALLED SIN.

We all disobey God, and the punishment for our sin is death. Thankfully, God had a plan from the beginning to save His people. We deserve to die for our sins, but the gospel says that God sent His Son, Jesus, to take our place. Jesus, who never sinned, died on the cross for us. Three days later, He came alive again! If we believe this good news and trust Jesus to save us, God forgives us, and we can live forever with Him.

**WHEN WE TRUST IN JESUS,
GOD CHANGES OUR HEARTS.**

He forgives us, makes us clean, and sends His Spirit to live inside us. He makes us His sons and daughters. He protects, loves, and cares for us. In response, we want to live in a way that makes Him happy. Doing good things doesn't save us. We don't obey God to make Him love us. He loves us always and forever! Instead, we obey God because we love Him.

WE CAN LEARN MORE ABOUT GOD AND WHAT HE LOVES THROUGH THE MOST IMPORTANT BOOK OF ALL, THE BIBLE.

The Bible tells us that one day, Jesus is coming again to make everything right. He will wipe away all our tears, and there will be no more pain or sadness. He will make everything good again.

If you trust in Jesus, don't keep this good news to yourself.
Tell someone about Jesus today!

Thank You

for studying God's
Word with us!

connect with us
@THEDAILYGRACECO @DAILYGRACEPODCAST

contact us
INFO@THEDAILYGRACECO.COM

share
#THEDAILYGRACECO

visit us online
WWW.THEDAILYGRACECO.COM